MONASTERY OF ST. ALPHONSUS
REDEMPTORISTINE NUNS
LIGUORI, MISSOURI

266
B

D0421816

Happy Those Who Believe

alba house ■ DIVISION OF THE SOCIETY OF ST. PAUL
STATEN ISLAND, N. Y. 10314

Happy Those Who Believe

266
BR

Bernard Bro, O.P.

Original title: Heureux de croire
Published by Les Editions du Cerf, Paris

Translated by John M. Morriss

Nihil Obstat:
Daniel V. Flynn, J.C.D.
Censor Librorum

Imprimatur:
Joseph P. O'Brien, S.T.D.
Vicar General, Archdiocese of New York
November 21, 1969

The nihil obstat and imprimatur are official declarations that a book or pamphlet is free of doctrinal or moral error. No implication is contained therein that those who have granted the nihil obstat and imprimatur agree with the contents, opinions or statements expressed.

Copyright 1970 by the Society of St. Paul, 2187 Victory Blvd., Staten Island, New York, 10314.

Library of Congress Catalog Card Number: 72-110593

SBN: 8189-0164-0

Designed, printed and bound in the U.S.A. by the Pauline Fathers and Brothers, 2187 Victory Blvd., Staten Island, N.Y. 10314 as part of their communications apostolate.

To My Friends Of Gordon
To My Friends Of Saint-Severin

CONTENTS

PART I

PART II

part 1

INTRODUCTION

WHERE DO WE BEGIN?

What Are Your Feelings on Sunday Morning?

We are sometimes asked questions for which we are automatically inclined to say "thank you." Some can hurt, while others can liberate. But I feel the need to offer my sincere thanks for, without knowing it, you, the reader, by the simple fact of your having opened this book, have raised a fundamental question: *What does it mean "to believe"?*

> Even for a priest, the occasion does not often arise when one is faced with a question that concerns this essential point. I have in mind the comment of a Marxist who one day said: "What escapes us Marxists is what you Christians must feel on Sunday morning." Behind this remark was a question that said more than a hundred books. What do I feel on Sunday morning? Here you are raising the question: "What can you say about your faith?" it is an opportunity to return to the essence of things.

A Wall Is a Wall

The poem of a sixteen-year-old boy, on the threshold of life, serves well as an introduction:

Between man and love
There is a woman
Between man and woman
There is the world
Between man and the world
There is a wall.

The evil assail it
The strong climb it
Others remain in its shadow.
For some a wall is a wall
They skirt it without thinking of
    evil . . .
Or of God.

To those imprisoned everything is a
    wall.
Even an open door.

Perhaps there is a wall between God and us: "To those imprisoned everything is a wall, even an open door." This raises two questions. Where do we begin? What are our attitudes? Does not each one of us more or less build his own wall? Do we not allow a wall to come between God and ourselves? Secondly, do our own attitudes constitute a wall? Or are they not the *normal* starting-off point of faith?

A STRANGE PROCESSION

What are our real attitudes? Let us question ourselves above and beyond theories, ideas, and impressions.

The Fearful Ones

Three banal observations can be made. First, no matter who we are, at certain times we experience uncertainty, a feeling of fear, even confusion. This is not reserved to the Church or to Christians. In economics, politics, in every branch of human thought and science, we are nowadays much more aware of the limitation of ideas and theories. Men can no longer rely solely on systems of thought. They have learned that ideologies are not definitive answers. Let us recall the questions surrounding the phenomenon of heart transplants: When does death really take place? When does a person have the right to perform such an operation? These are not simple questions nor is it easy to take a position. And all of us have witnessed those remarkable television programs where two groups of men confront each other, reaching radically different conclusions on the problem of the atomic bomb or the nuclear striking force: doctors, physicists, former government officials, all very sincere men. It soon becomes clear to the thinking man that ideas are no longer enough to bring security, yet security is an indispensable element in man's life.

Those who have lived in or traveled through Sweden, which is assumed to be ten or twenty years ahead of other countries — a civilization marked by an intelligent organization of things, a certain well-being, a certain system of justice — have been left with an impression: coming from outside, one can sense not happiness or peace, but a terrible need for protection and above all the desire to avoid any type of questioning. Not too many questions, please; first of all, we must have security.

But we learn that faith does not simplify things and that God himself poses a question. We know the usury of words: what meaning do we give to words like

sin,

immortality of the soul,

God's justice,

God's presence,

etc., etc., etc?

What dogmas

e involved here?   What morality?

the tired ones

Even without fear we experience *fatigue*. No need to stress the fact: living conditions, work environment, the rapidity of change, and the inverse effect of improved communications sometimes weigh very heavily on us. Today in electronics a generation of computers lasts three years. And in every branch of learning, such as medicine, physics, even theology, a person must renew his studies at least once every seven to ten years. The vastness of information fatigues and overwhelms us. Our missals are outdated the day we buy them!

Those of you who have the responsibility or the joy of a country home know very well that to maintain a home you must anticipate every year one percent of the total value in repairs or upkeep. Otherwise you run the risk of being overwhelmed by serious problems such as roofing. On certain days, overcome with lassitude, we may even ask ourselves whether we still have the operational minimum to maintain our faith. People become resigned to things. Just as children grow up and give their parents the impression of avoiding them, we too sometimes have the impression that ideas are getting away from us, that it is fatiguing to pursue them, and that people no longer bother about such things. We are in a sense on a train, no longer knowing where it is going, and no longer having the strength to change stations.

The Somnambulists

Even if a person is not uncertain, disturbed by insecurity, or tired, there is a third attitude which we all more or less experience. It is what St. Paul has in mind when he talks of our somnolence.

It would be incorrect and very wrong to be pessimistic toward the modern-day world. We are aware of a general good will, a fount of good will which is surprising. But such good will is not at all incompatible with a certain state of somnolence or, to use St. Paul's image, with a certain state of *somnambulist*. People have religious attitudes and habits. Not only are they generally not "against" things (the horizon of their life may even be taken up by explicitly religious works and activities, such as the apostolate, the liturgy, etc.) but people are often genuinely concerned about others or about the Church *provided it does not inconvenience them too much, provided they are not faced with essential questions, and provided that God does not arouse them.* We are of good will toward God provided we do not have to make a decision or an option of faith. We experience this sometimes with anxiety before the reception of certain sacraments: we do not want to be stirred up. We do not want to make a real choice of faith. We are very clever in justifying this somnambulistic state. We convince ourselves that we must "adapt ourselves" and be "closer to the real world." We rationalize that the Church is still "too far removed from the world." Or else we feel our mission is to defend the Truth, as if the Truth needed to be defended. Everything is fine provided we do not have to answer for ourselves.

What could arouse us, such as the influence of atheism in the Third World, passes through our clerical scleroses and is translated by us in a way to put us to sleep, to sleep so that we do not have to decide to listen or not listen to Jesus Christ. We "have" faith, but possess it as a thing and not as the passion of our life.

Certain people, who decide to eliminate faith from their life, have an energy whose tenacity can show us, in a negative or contrary way, what it means to get out of our somnambulistic state. I remember the expression of a woman who in the midst of her memoirs says: "I had succeeded in doing without the idea of God, but I had not yet succeeded in no longer needing salvation, in no longer needing to be saved." And we might ask ourselves if we have any real eagerness to reach the decisions and options demanded by faith? People become lethargic amid habits. As in the case of an iceberg, we are only concerned about the ten percent that is visible and not the ninety percent that is submerged.

BECAUSE OF SLEEP AND FEAR

You will say to me: "Somnambulists, fearful men, tired men, what a procession!" But do we not all more or less experience fear, lassitude, and sluggishness? Is this not the "wall" between God and ourselves?

But (and this is our second question) we must ask ourselves: Is it normal to be tired, to know fear? And must we turn our impressions over and over to learn that this is the normal starting-point of faith?

"To those imprisoned everything is a wall, even an open door." Instead of being vexed by such fear, such fatigue, or such somnolence, should we not ask ourselves how faith stimulates us simply *because* we are fearful or too exhausted?

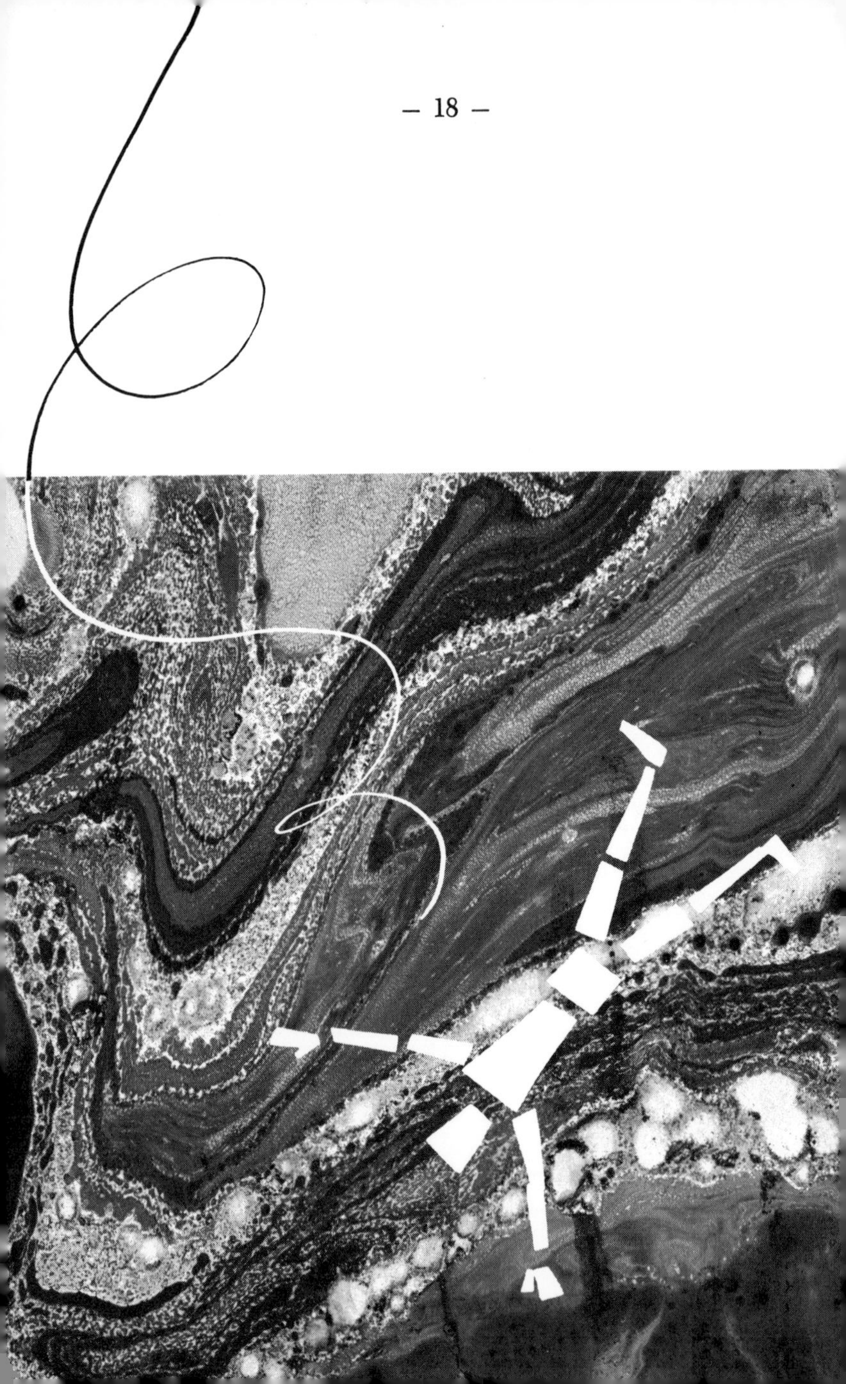

Perhaps you remember the incident that happened to the five Norwegians of Kon Tiki. They had decided to journey through the 3,700 miles of the Pacific Ocean from the shores of Chile to the Easter Islands, pushed by the wind, on a raft provided with a simple sail and shed. But in the middle of the ocean, one fine day, one of them wanted to take a dip. He dove down into the water and swam a long distance. He was not aware, or rather he became aware only too late, of the violence of the wind. The raft moved off irrevocably into the distance. The swimmer became exhausted and weary from his desperate efforts to save himself. He was about to perish.

One of his comrades spotted him and quickly ran up the sail. But the wind was still too strong and the raft continued to move away.

Suddenly an idea came to him of the only practical way that he could save his companion. He took a rope and threw it: the man who was about to perish was able to grab it and be pulled back on the raft.

Aren't we somewhat like that tired swimmer who wore himself out flailing the waves, who struggled to save himself by his own efforts, and who experienced fear?

True, when we are exhausted, we can think only of our own fatigue; or when somnambulistic, not see that the raft is moving away; or when afraid, have doubts about the person who is on the raft, and who alone can save us. The Gospel reminds us that there is someone — faith is, first of all, that — who can throw us a rope and it proposes the mooring that can save us. "He shall call upon me, and I will answer him; I will be with him in distress" (Ps 90, 15). This faith, which is ours, is first of all the recognition of a call, a call connected with this need to be saved which exists in us. Next, it is an encounter and, finally, a change of life, as clear-cut as the one proposed to us to come out of the water.

"TO THOSE IMPRISONED EVERY-
THING IS A WALL, EVEN AN
OPEN DOOR." DOES FAITH
MAKE US FEEL THAT ALL OUR
WALLS CAN DISAPPEAR, EVEN
THOSE WE IMAGINE? DOES IT
TEACH US THAT OUR FATIGUE,
OUR LASSITUDE ITSELF, HAS A
MEANING? AND IS IT TRUE
THAT A PERSON CAN BE HAPPY
IN THE BELIEF THAT THERE IS
SOMEONE, SOMEONE ON THE
OTHER SIDE, AND THEREFORE
THAT WE DO NOT HAVE TO BE
AFRAID OF BEING EXHAUSTED,
FEARFUL, OR SOMNOLENT? IS
THERE REALLY SOMEONE ON
THE OTHER SIDE OF ALL
HUMAN WALLS, SOMEONE WHO
OPENS THE DOOR FOR US, AND
WHO IS CHRIST?

NOTE

The Three Moments of Faith

In the following three chapters, we will examine each of the great "moments" of faith. We do not mean to separate three distinct instants. We must understand the word "moment" in the Latin or German sense of the word, that is, as the permanent aspect of a reality, and not in the strictly chronological or temporal sense.

It is evident that this call, this encounter, and this attitude are incomprehensible if we separate them one from the other. There is reciprocity between them: faith is *at one and the same time* an attraction of God, the commitment of one's being to Christ, and an illumination. In addition, faith is something lived according to a variety of temperaments. It is obvious that St. Paul (and later on Pascal and Kierkegaard, for example) emphasized strongly the dissatisfaction with self from which the true life of faith gradually matured. St. Matthew, St. Mark, and St. Luke emphasized perhaps more the encounter and unconditional commitment of oneself to Christ. St. John did not cease to remind us that since God was light, faith was an illumination and renewal of our point of view. But for everyone, faith is at one and the same time a calling, an encounter, and a viewpoint. Behind this trilogy will be found the wonderful theology of faith.

Likewise we could very easily recall how the lives of all the saints — and of all converts — have been marked by these three moments. Charles de Foucauld saw the separation between his life and the true life, and after his encounter with Christ and the change in his outlook, he went from one calling to the next, from one encounter to the next, and finally to martyrdom. As early as the age of four, Thérèse of Lisieux felt the call, saw the disproportion between the life to which God summoned her and the limitations of the life she knew. Her struggle lasted fifteen years and in the last eight months of her life the struggle and calling began again. Claudel started with an illumination, with Rimbaud, then the encounter at Notre-Dame, and four years of summoning before he was finally disarmed.

According to what I am told,
I am the son of man and woman;
This astonishes me ....
I thought I was more.

Lautréamont

I
A Calling

When the ducks fly away

This is how one of the intellectual masters of our time, an author who is apparently the most read among "paperback" authors, in France, described one of the most decisive moments of life — without question, the most decisive: the moment when man recognizes a calling. He described it in a parable, the parable of the ducks. He was painting the scene of that period in autumn when the ducks and the wild geese fly South.

At the time of migrations, a strange tide is seen in the regions where ducks and geese are in great number. The domestic birds are, as it were magnetized by their great triangular formations and they themselves attempt an awkward flight but fall within a few feet. The call of the wild has aroused in the strongest way possible some strange vestige. For a moment the farm ducks are changed into migratory birds. In that little hard head of theirs, where small images of tides, worms, and hens whirl about,  there appear continental distances, the thirst for sea winds, and the vast expanse of the oceans. And the duck staggers from left to right in his fenced-in enclosure, caught by this sudden passion and not knowing where it is taking him and by this vast love the object of which is unknown to him. Likewise, man, gripped by evidence he is uncertain of, discovers the emptiness of his daily occupations as well as of the soft pleasures of his domestic life. But he is unable to give a name to this sudden truth. This soul-stirring call no doubt torments all men. But domestic security has choked off the part in us that could hear it. We hardly stir. We flutter our wings two or three times, and then fall down again in our courtyard. We are reasonable beings. We are afraid of letting go of our little prey. The domestic duck was unaware that his tiny head was large enough to contain oceans.

This parable, written by someone who did not call himself explicitly a Christian — and that is even more interesting — puts us face to face with the beginning of faith, its first movement.

An impression of discomfort

We are often disconcerted by the way in which faith is manifested in our lives, since most of the time we are unaware of what is involved, or else we think we know — it is only after the fact that we realize that it was a question of faith. This first real, profound manifestation of God's life in the life of man is a grace which arouses and disturbs man. It is like a "cry" in us which we cannot explain and which returns even when we think it has gone away — as with the ducks at the time of the migrations. And such a cry disturbs us since we do not understand that faith is involved. The impression which summarizes this perhaps best is a feeling of discomfort: there are questions which arise in us, which surpass us, and we sense that we are unable to find a *definitive* response for them.

Why, for example, do we have this tenacious need in our lives to love or to be loved? Why is there such a thing as time, the past, failure, separation?

Nothing is ever acquired by man,
either his strength or his weakness or his heart.
And when he thinks he is opening
out his arms, his shadow is that of a cross.
And when he thinks he is holding his happiness,
he crushes it.
His life is a strange
and pitiful divorce.

We are well aware that we are unable to provide definitive answers. This is where man's greatness lies; only the mind can do that: to perceive the separation between what he is, what he does, what he gives himself, and what he wants, what he can hope for. Even in the lower courtyard I can look beyond the gate; I can hear a call (perhaps I cannot follow it, but at least I can hear it) to sense this question which arises in me:

According to what I am told,

I am the son of man and woman;

This astonishes me . . .

I thought I was more.

It must be said that if this is our grandeur, it is also our misery: because we are capable of making ourselves, little by little, deaf to such calls. This is the tragic aspect of the grandeur of the mind. Each of us succeeds perfectly, if he so wishes, in suffocating the questions that disturb him, in anesthetizing them. "Domestic security has choked off the part in us that could hear the call. We hardly stir. We flutter our wings two or three times, and then fall down again in our courtyard. We are reasonable beings."

None of us can prevent himself from developing a thirst in his life, a thirst for light, for truth, for achievement. But if we all know this thirst, many of us also succeed in extinguishing it. Finally, we have a thirst for happiness, but we are afraid of being thirsty.

Because you were a man of desire

And what do we see in the Gospel? We forever find ourselves before men who seem to be in a state of questioning, a state of waiting, a state of dissatisfaction. We have the impression that a great flight is taking place above them. They are in a state of subterranean preparation. They will realize, after the fact, that it was the work of God, that it was the generous complicity of God, in their lives.

Let us consider John the Baptist, the first one who sensed the call. He was in prison, finishing out his life there, yet our Lord did not offer to take him out of prison, contrary to what he could expect. No, he offered him a call, a hope, so that he could emerge from his interior prison: "The poor hear the Good News; the blind see; the deaf hear."

And as for the other men in the Gospel? Consider Zacchaeus, who struggled against the prison of his conscience; Mary Magdalene and the Samaritan woman, who struggled against the prison of their heart. . . . All sensed a call. They were in a state of dissatisfaction. We would not invent, we would never have dared imagine, these preparatory cries of the Old Testament when God said to Daniel: "I came to you because you were a man of desire." And in Jeremias: "I will put them in anguish so that they may find me." In all these cases we see people in a state of dissatisfaction, who, precisely because they are in such a state, have sensed that there were obstacles to overcome.

This grace of calling is at the same time a grace of struggle, whether it is a struggle against the exterior conditions of their life (being a Samaritan or Publican was not conducive to hearing the call of Christ) or simply against interior conditions (for St. Peter, doubt about himself) or even against religious or intellectual convictions. When he talks about faith, St. Paul stresses this last point: even an abstract religious conviction can act as a screen to hide the call and invitation of God. St. Paul speaks out against the false assurances given by circumcision (for example, in the Epistle to the Philippians, chapter 3, and in the Epistle to the Romans, chapter 10): "But the things that were gain to me, these, for the sake of Christ, I have counted loss. For his sake I have suffered the loss of all things, that I may gain Christ and be found in him, not having a justice of my own, which is from the Law, but that which is from faith in Christ, the justice from God based upon faith." And he adds a phrase which we almost always interpret in a gross, contrary way, understanding it as if St. Paul was thinking of debauchery. But this is not what he had in mind; it was circumcision, a condition in which some people placed their assurance: "For many walk, of whom I have told you often and now tell you even weeping, that they are enemies of the cross of Christ. Their end is ruin, their god is the belly, their glory is in their shame. Beware of such evil workers, beware of the mutilation."

It is true, a person can say no to God's call. He can refuse his offer. We see it in the Gospel: the

rich
young
man
says
no.

And in the parable of the banquet, we feel Christ's anguish before the alibis that we ourselves can give.

Those invited to the banquet have very good alibis, excellent reasons, for not responding to the call: a daughter to marry off, a field, just bought, to survey, a pair of oxen to try out.

In other words, all the reasons are summarized in two great reasons: family life or work.

But if God's call is directed only to those who have neither family nor work, who then will be able to respond?

IF YOU EXIST, GIVE ME LIGHT

What do we make of this call? The remark of a great moviemaker summarizes best the twofold aspect of this first grace of faith, which is also a grace of simulation, questioning, and a call in the name of enlightenment. Henri-Georges Cluzot, producer of *Mystère Picasso*, *Diaboliques* and *La Verité*, once remarked in an interview:

> Everything starts off with a feeling of spiritual discomfort. The test occasioned by the death of Vera, my wife, was terrible, but I never thought of seeking consolation in the idea that people would become reunited in another world. No, at that time, I was very far removed from the hope of the next world. But I felt that the philosophy of the absurd, after having carried me along a certain distance, came upon an impasse. Then I told myself that if I could not find a supernatural means of salvation, I had to find one for the here and now, within me, in this life. That is, a way of being on terms with myself, without asking for any other reward. Then I began to read. I read and read and, by accident, came across the work of Simone Weil. Through the example of her life, her explanation of evil and the suffering of the innocent, through her faith,

through her way of loving her neighbor more than herself, through all that, I began to think that perhaps there was a way. Her commentary on the Our Father, which she recited, overcome with fatigue, in the vineyards of the free zone at the start of the Occupation, the diary she kept in a factory, all that penetrated me. I felt personally spoken to. I discovered that faith was not only something which can be discussed in the abstract, intellectually. Then I began with a very vague prayer, which was not even the prayer of Abraham for when Abraham said: "I am there" before God, he believed completely in a single God. As for me, I was not there. I was before an unknown God. I said: "If you exist, give me light." I believe that I committed the true sin when I was fifteen or sixteen-years-old: it was the sin against the spirit, which is a reflection of original sin. It is wanting to be oneself by oneself.

Then the interviewer asked him: "All alone?" And Henri-Georges Cluzot answered.

"Yes, all alone."

"Lord, if you exist, give me light." Wanting to be oneself by oneself, is for us the same temptation. God calls us gradually, from one level to the next. He attracts us in some mysterious way. We become aware of it after it is done. But it is often very simple: our conscience is stirred, or becomes uncomfortable, with very specific points of departure which deceive us because they are too unassuming, too close at hand. We do not believe that faith is already there, that it is calling us, and that, as the Epistle to the Romans says, God "stirs up our jealousy." In a discrete way he proposes something better, a surpassing of ourselves, within our conscience. For Abraham — and Abraham did not know what it meant —: to have a son; for St. Peter: to become a fisher of men. We then learn that discomfort is not the last word. But God remains disconcerting, so discrete is he. He arouses us, stirs us up, but we are always free to prefer something else and not pay attention.

Such is the second aspect of this beginning of faith, which is not only a calling, an attraction to surpass ourselves, but something which provokes us to a struggle, a struggle against ourselves. It is the same force that gripped St. Peter, and which fortified John the Baptist, a grace of contention against all scleroses, against loss of confidence, against interior weaknesses.

Coming home from work, some poor fishwives, surprised by a violent storm, left their pails outside and sought refuge in the garden of a rich landowner. The latter received them warmly, provided them with a meal, and allowed them to rest in a great veranda, in the midst of magnificent flowers that filled the air with a sweet fragrance. The women lay down in this scented paradise, but were unable to fall asleep. They missed something which was a part of their lives and which they could not do without. Realizing what they were lacking, one of them got up and looked for the fish pails and brought them into the veranda. Then, once again under the influence of the familiar scent, they soon fell into a deep sleep.

Who can pretend that he does not have his own "pail of fish," that is, the collection of plans, thoughts, and images that are well known to us, and which we have no desire of giving up. We hold firm to the image of ourselves which we create and which we do not want to abandon. In no way do we want to give up the privilege, for example, of being able to develop ourselves according to the manner we have chosen.

Hearing a call is the first moment* of faith, which is so wonderful when we see it appearing: accepting for itself a way different from the one we have been given. Accepting for itself another plan, another rule, another image than the one we create for ourselves, and agreeing not to depart from it. We are well aware that when enlightenment comes from someone else, it is not easy to accept. Take, for example, the normal reaction to questions or criticisms regarding one's fiancée. Or that of an adolescent who, at the threshold of life, had constructed an idea of what he wants to do in terms of a career, when someone else lets him know that he is not realistic. Or when we feel that the idea which our superiors have of us does not coincide perfectly with what we think of ourselves. When someone else suggests or proposes another idea, another way of doing something, how inclined we are to reach quickly for our "pail of fish" once again!

Isn't it the same with God? The gift of faith is a grace of contention, but first of all against ourselves and not against others. This is the first turnaround of faith: *to have chosen* (for it is a choice, a decision) *not to be contented with the idea that one has of oneself.*

---

* See p. 24

The Favorite of Psychiatrists

If we were to ask psychiatrists who their favorites are, I think that they would generally give the same answer. They would tell us that those whom they prefer are those who peacefully accept the separation that exists between what they think they are and the calling that they sense. As if there were basically two categories among men: those who know that the idea a person makes for himself is something relative and can be examined by means of the light that comes from elsewhere and which one yearns for; and then those who resist, who refuse to be enlightened.

No doubt, this is the peace, the joy, of being happy to believe. It is the secret quality of the joy, of the first moment, of faith: knowing and accepting the fact that someone else has charge of the plan, the idea, that we can have for ourselves. But not only in the manner of psychiatrists: no, he is in charge in the name of some-

thing positive, *in the name of a calling,* in the name of
the place he has reserved for us in his plan. Sometimes
I pause with a feeling of great joy before that passage in
the Gospel when our Lord says: "Rejoice, not in having
performed miracles (that is, in having done things that
conform to the idea which you make for yourselves),
but *in the fact that your name is written in heaven.*"
This joy, which had to be that of St. Peter against all
his prisons, his interior doubts, like that of Abraham or
John the Baptist when they responded to the call, when
they simply agreed that someone else would be in charge
of the image, the idea, which they had of themselves.

"To be happy to believe." Yes, we can know the joy
contained in the calling which we sometimes feel: someone has written our name in heaven and it is that name
which is summoning us.

But let us not forget that each morning a "pail of
fish" awaits us.

Go, seek your husband.

don't have a husband.

He told me everything I did.

II

An Encounter

We can hear many times the conversation of the Samaritan woman with Christ or the narrative of the disciples of Emmaus (undoubtedly one of the most beautiful selections in world literature) without realizing their full meaning. I will admit that this was my situation. I had often heard a reading of these passages and was already in the religious life, when a parable was told to me; a parable more simple than the pages of this book, but one which enabled me to understand better the mystery and depth of these particular passages.

Respond or Else Die.

It was the parable of the labyrinth. The ancients had imagined the development of human existence, the scenario of our life, in terms of a labyrinth. With easy moments, simple, straightforward passages, where one sees the way and advances quickly; with other moments when one has the impression of going back on his steps, wasting time, being brought back to the starting-off point, and getting lost in detours or impasses.

But, according to the parable, in this labyrinth every man was led to encounter the most unusual creature imaginable: it had the face of a man, a very beautiful body, and, to indicate his strength, the wings of an eagle. To each man, this creature asked a question; and putting his hand on the shoulder of each one, the sphinx ended his question with these words: "Respond or else die."

It is true that our life is like a labyrinth, with its simple, easy, straightforward moments and then its other moments when we are somewhat lost, when we have the impression of going back on our steps, marking time, or else standing at impasses or detours.

It is also true that there are moments when we feel we are almost above ourselves, or in the helter skelter of our existence, we feel that something is being proposed to us, as if an event were going to take place in our life. Moments which cannot easily be expressed in words, which cannot be reduced to a simple expression, for they are too rich. Moments which we designate by a very beautiful word, perhaps one of the most beautiful in the French language: an "encounter" (*rencontre*). This will help us to understand the second aspect, the second moment, in the life of faith: an encounter, that moment when we have discovered or understood someone, and when we have thereby understood ourselves better; that moment when, because of the intervention of someone else, we feel, as it were, larger, more lucid.

If we reflect for an instant, we will realize how few encounters there are in our lives: a parent, a teacher, a professor, a friend ... perhaps even a child. There are not many encounters in our lives, moments when we have been placed above ourselves and from which we emerge larger, having understood a little better who we were.

"Respond or else die": like the Samaritan woman, like the disciples of Emmaus, we sense that we can either accept or else refuse a little bit more of death. This is a privilege of our conscience, which cannot ignore it.

What Do You Seek?

What Do You Seek?

What Do You Seek

What is the Gospel all about? If it were necessary to summarize in a word what the Gospel is, we could perhaps say that it is but the history of a series of encounters. Let us consider the life of a man like St. Peter: it is a life set in the framework of a few encounters. In the beginning, there is the question so typical of Christ: "What do you seek?" The first encounter: "What do you seek?" Then, right afterwards, the movement of fear in Peter in the second encounter: "Lord, depart from me, I am a sinner." He is still afraid. But then, after the multiplication of the loaves, his trust increases. It is the third encounter: "To whom would we go, for you have the words of eternal life?"

Finally the last three encounters, so simple and decisive: before the Passion, Peter affirms his confidence before all the others: "I will follow you no matter where." Shortly thereafter there is the betrayal and the encounter with Christ's look. Finally, right after the Resurrection, the last encounter, the ultimate question: "Peter, do you love me? — do you love me more?" Thus was Peter's life set in the framework of a few encounters with Christ.

Everywhere in the Gospel we observe the same thing: a widow, a young man, Mary Magdalene, the Samaritan woman, Zacchaeus, a man praying for his deceased daughter, young husbands. . . . Each time we notice two characteristics of the encounter in the Gospel, of every encounter with Christ: it is at the time very simple, almost banal, and yet decisive.

It is a sign for our own encounter with God.

Penetrating Thoughts

These encounters are simple, yet they are also disconcerting. There is always, as it were, a certain element of surprise. God is the unexpected one: for example, with the man born blind, it is not a matter of chance that the encounter takes place on the Sabbath, the day when healings were not to be performed. With the Samaritan woman, Christ is one with whom one does not come into contact, the stranger, and it is he who invites the encounter. With the Apostles, the moment could not be more poorly chosen: at the end of a night after they had worked hard. At the end of a day's work, people are on edge, and more so when they have worked throughout the night. That is the moment that Christ chose, apparently the worst possible moment. Even when one had a premonition, God remains the unexpected one. As Kierkegaard said in talking about the pages of the Gospel, when they provoke us toward an encounter: "These are thoughts that strike us in the back."

It is surprising, and at the same time what is proposed is extremely simple. One senses it at each encounter, for example, between Christ and the Samaritan woman, that moment when the dialogue is under way. It is simply a question of *accepting the truth*. With some modesty Christ proposes it. He does not accuse her, he does not even make her blush, he simply says: "Please, go seek your husband"; and she at once answers: "I don't have a husband." He says: "You have spoken truly, you have had five husbands, and the man with whom you live is not your husband."

●●

This is what brings the encounter together: *agreeing to being recognized for what one is, agreeing to be loved for what one is*. This is the essence of the second grace of faith: *accepting a word of love, mercy, pardon, which offers us light*.

●●

It is an incredibly simple thing and at the same time always decisive. "Respond or else die." In effect, Christ proposes that a person truly give himself to him. He makes the proposal and then waits. Nothing happens unless a person truly gives himself to him. We see this in the case of the Samaritan woman, in contrast to what happens in the case of Nicodemus or the disciples of Emmaus, when Christ regretfully remarks: "Hearts without intelligence, minds slow to believe." Another cure is significant of the waiting that Christ does and of our own difficulty in giving ourselves to him in a definitive, unconditional way. It is the case of the father who is unsure as to whether or not Christ would be able to cure his son. The father says (unfortunately the text is often incompletely translated): "If you can . . ." and Christ responds specifically: "If you can believe, all things are possible to him who believes" (Mark 9, 23).

But note, on the contrary, Christ's joy before the firm, definitive, unconditional trust of the centurion, of Zacchaeus. A Chinese proverb says: "He who seeks God and sells all that he has except for his last penny, is indeed foolish, for it is with the last penny that one gains possession of God." Is my trust firm? Is it unconditional? Am I putting myself in the hands of the Other Person? After all, it is quite normal: when someone loves somebody, he waits to see if a certain expression — a perfectly honest expression — appears in him.

God also waits for such an expression.

Such is the second moment of faith:

> *an unconditional giving*
> *of oneself to a word of mercy,*
> *to a word of love.*

What Attracts Man's Interest?

How do we live out these two aspects of every encounter? It is something very simple, and yet something that is decisive and unconditional. Basically, what attracts our interest in an encounter? It is not necessarily what the other person brings us. It is not, I think, first of all its utilitarian aspect. In spite of what is said in magazines or in advertising, is it really money or sex? I do not think so, despite the frequency with which these motives are stressed in this day and age.

This is not what interests man. It is something else. It is love. And *in love*
            it is the possibility
       of being accepted completely,
               of having one's true value recognized. If Mary Magdalene, if Zacchaeus had ceased growing and, in their mediocrity, experienced a certain distress, is it not because they realized they were no longer loved, because they no longer existed for someone who loved them? When Christ comes, he loves them as they are. And once again they begin to hope and therefore to grow. This is what will overwhelm Peter, Mary Magdalene, Zacchaeus, the Samaritan woman: being loved for what they are. This is the Good News of the encounter. God is love and the Christian is the man who believes that he has a right to love, that there is someone who loves us as we are.

But on one condition namely, that we truly give ourselves to him and that in this encounter we accept the fact that something irreversible, something unconditional, is involved. Father de Foucauld described it very well when speaking of his encounter with Christ:

> "As soon as I believed that there was a God, I realized that I could do nothing else but live for him alone. My religious vocation dates from the same hour as my faith."

And in the Gospel, the cure of the blind man of Bethsaida offers us one of the most telling episodes. A blind man is brought, "carried," to Christ. And the blind man reveals his misery to Christ, he cannot see, he cannot meet other people, he cannot move about by himself. Then Christ "took him by the hand" and "led him forth," and the blind man agreed, in the darkness, to walk through the village. The Gospel adds: Christ cures him *outside the village* and the blind man begins to see (Mark 8, 22). It is the same with us. Christ has taken us by the hand. And if we agree to pass through the entire village of our existence, as in the Gospel, with the same trust as that of the blind man, who agreed without questioning, without complaining, without trying to find his own way alongside his guide, then at the end we too shall see.

It depends on us, for we have that astonishing, yet awesome, power of establishing Christ as our savior. It is we who, by our attitude, enable God, as it were, to become God for us, to be a source, a giver, a Father. We are like children, who, if they wish, can frustrate the paternity of their parents, refuse it, or else take it at its word. As in the Gospel, we can take Christ at his word. It is not a question of seizing Christ but of being seized by him in the encounter. And if we agree to yield to him, it is we who will provide him with the opportunity to give himself to us, to recognize us, to love us.

This is when we will experience the fullness of the encounter and the joy of faith: "Respond or else die." We sense the joy of encounter in the Samaritan woman: "He told me everything I was." In this second movement there is, as it were, a turnaround of faith: not only is truth attained, not only are we recognized completely for what we are, but someone else takes charge of us, of me, and carries my life on his shoulders.

The Beloved One of Jalâl el Din Roûmi

A Mohammedan poet, a Persian mystic, said the same thing in a story that is one of the most beautiful love stories. It is the story of a fiancé who returns to his beloved. He knocks at the door once and from within a question is asked: "Who's there?" The fiancé answers: "Beloved, it is I, open up." But the door is not opened. Then the fiancé thinks a while, comes back a second time, and knocks. And again the same question from within: "Who's there?" Again the fiancé replies: "Beloved it is I, open up." But the door remains closed.

● Then, after a little more reflection, he comes back and knocks for the third time. Again the question from within: "Who's there?" This time he replies: "Beloved, it is you." Then the door is opened.

It is you, Lord, it is you. The same is also true of us in our faith. We accept this sublime fruit of encounter: to give ourselves to you. We accept the fact that it is you who enable us to give ourselves. Lord, it is you. It is you who give us confidence, you who enable us to hope, you who, in times of fear, doubt, and weakness, give us hope. It is you who restore my youth, it is you who are my true measure.

Such is the turnaround of faith. I believe because someone else carries me, because someone else loves me, because someone else gives me back my dignity, and that changes everything. "Respond or else die." Yes, that is my last penny, at the moment when I am afraid of abandoning myself. It is you who give me my strength, you who give me your strength, Lord; it is you who give me your hope, you who give me your certitude.

and í saw

III

A LOOK

In a recent chronicle, the following passage appeared:
"A painter tells me that he was drafted during World War II. His duty was to guard the railroad tracks in a region that overflowed with beauty. He was given as a companion a butcher's assistant. Since the painter often interrupted his watch to appreciate the surrounding countryside, the assistant asked him:

What are you doing,
standing there?

I'm looking at the
landscape.

And when you look at the
landscape, what do you
see?

The most beautiful thing
after the human face.

That's funny, said the
assistant, I look at
landscapes to no avail.
I have never seen anything
other than the oxen,
sheep, or pigs that are
there."

The way we look at things is something we have in ourselves; it is what is most personal and perhaps most precious in man.

Our outlook enables us to understand better the third moment of faith, the ultimate and decisive instant in the life of faith. Let us pause to find out what our outlook, or more exactly our change of outlook, means.

When You Look at the Countryside, What Do You See?

People are affected by the way other people see things, their way of envisaging the universe, objects, and life. The painter and the butcher's assistant each saw something different. In the cure of the blind man, St. John notes this very well; he presents groups of very typical men: apostles, parents, Pharisees, the blind man himself, and each reacts differently.

A person develops his own way of looking at things or else he deforms it. The possibility of educating or deforming his way of looking at things is perhaps one of the most important, the most astonishing — sometimes the most tragic — powers that man possesses. It takes a long time to fashion it, a long time to change it.

One day, in the course of a walk with a friend in archeology, in that region situated between the valley of the Serein and the valley of the Yonne (which contains the most important quadrilateral in France: Auxerre, Vézelay, Avallon, Pontigny), I was enraptured by the beauty of it all. A mound, a ditch, a small plot of ground, and my friend would lead me along and say: "Come,

come see." And there, like a flower in the soil, appeared an old Roman coin, a potsherd, a piece of pottery: vestiges of a Gallo-Roman villa. I had not noticed anything. The folds of land meant nothing to me. Yet he had seen it all.

You have certainly already experienced this in the month of September, for example, when driving in a car with a hunter. His look moves to the right and left. And he sees things: a partridge, a hare. I do not notice anything . . . but would prefer that he keep his eyes on the road.

The look of an archeologist, a painter, a butcher, a hunter. . . . Put them in the same countryside, and each sees something different. And in life we know the surprise that parents sometimes experience: Why, of two children, does one have a spontaneously kind, naturally happy look, and the other not? Why?

This look belongs to us, and we are responsible for it; yet we are not so desirous of seeing things as they are, but rather as we would like them to be. This is so apparent in the episode of the man born blind: the Pharisees and the man's parents would like to have seen something else.

In the Gospel, we have noted, the men who appear before Christ are always men in a state of dissatisfaction, in a state of questioning, men who have felt a calling in themselves, and the thing that affects their life is an encounter. But the fruit of that encounter, its success, is always a certain change in outlook.

We will now observe that this change involves a struggle and that faith is the marvelous victory of light.

FIXED LOOKS

Our Lord tries to modify men's ways of looking at things. He does not always succeed. Consider Judas, when he encounters Christ and Mary Magdalene with the jar of perfume: Judas does not change his outlook toward money. When Simon the Pharisee encounters Christ and the sinful woman, he does not change his outlook toward sin. And consider the Pharisees and parents during the episode of the man born blind. It was a very important thing for the parents: it was a question of their son. And yet they do not change their attitude toward Jesus. The son changes his own. He sees. He believes.

And likewise the father and mother of Jesus, in the very first episode reported about Christ's life, when as a child he is found teaching in the Temple. He begins by asking them to change their outlook:

"Did you not

know that I must be about
my Father's business?"

In contrast to the viewpoints of the Pharisees, Judas, or Simon, we see the viewpoints that open up, are transfigured, are converted, and are transformed.

In our own life as well as in the Gospel, we notice that there is one obstacle, to final conversion, to the life of faith, and therefore a struggle takes place. In the Gospel as well as in life, there are always fixed outlooks, restricted viewpoints, that are opposed to each other. Let us also note that in the Gospel the outlooks that refused to change were always those of sad men. This is understandable inasmuch as they do not judge reality by what is, but on the basis of their own ideas, "principles," and prejudices. The Pharisees were convinced they had good principles. A person judges things on the basis of the eyeglasses he has made for himself.

OPINION IS POWERFUL

Man's outlook is a powerful
force. So also is opinion. The
Sadducees, the Pharisees, the Romans
were all convinced that they were right.
This is the only point where they came
together: all were in agreement on destroying
Christ, on crucifying him. A look like an opinion,
can be most destructive. Looking at a newspaper, in
time of war, we realize how strong the elements of
opinion can be. This is what killed Christ. Opinion,
outlook. Do we act otherwise when we speak, think, or
make judgments about the Church? How narrowminded
we sometimes are! It is difficult for us to call
things by their name. There is a battle involved
in making room for something other than oneself
and holding firm against oneself so that reality
and truth may rule over us. This involves not
defending ideas, one's own ideas which are still
only intermediary ones, but agreeing to things
as they are, as God sees them. When John XXIII
was elected pope, many people thought he was
a provincial peasant. And when
Monsignor Veuillot was named arch-
bishop of Paris, he provoked the exact
same reaction (although now people speak in
quite different terms). ● Men are limited and
reduce everything to the level of their own limitations. Let us recall the cutting remark of the father who
expressed God's will in the parable of the vinegrowers:

"Must your eye be bad because I am good?" We accuse other people and other things for what befalls us. Basically we are afraid of changing our way of looking at things because we are afraid of love.

Our Lord did not hide from us the fact that this was and would be the decisive struggle of our life and that we would be judged on this point. Let us remember the great scene of the Last Judgment, when men, in astonishment, would ask Christ: "Lord, when did we see you hungry or thirsty, as a stranger or naked, sick or a prisoner, and not help you?" They are completely surprised and dumbfounded. They had not recognized him. They had not "seen." They had not changed their way of looking at things.

The life of St. John Bosco contains a very typical episode of this transformation of outlook, of this kind of struggle.

If We Had Known That He Was A Saint

A short time before his death, St. John Bosco had to spend three weeks in Paris. He asked to stay in the rectory of a large church in the center of Paris. He was received there and was given a garret on the sixth floor. When a short time after his death the process of canonization was started, those who had seen him during his lifetime and especially those who had seen him living away from home (since a person is freer away from home, no longer being under the constraint of his environment) were summoned. The vicar of Paris offered this response, as candid as it was awesome: "Naturally, if we knew he was a saint, we would not have put him on the sixth floor...."

"Lord, when did we see you?" They had not recognized him.

This is the decisive battle of our faith, this struggle between darkness and light. That is where the decisive grace of faith, the ultimate grace, enters in: To be able to look at the world, at other people, at things, at oneself, as Christ sees them. To look at God as Christ looks at him. What an extraordinary liberation for us, as it was for the man born blind: "Who is it, Lord?-It is I." To look with the look of Christ. Faith gives us Jesus not only as object and as light, but also as a way of looking at things. This victory is the victory of our life.

THE HISTORY OF THE SAINTS has preserved for us an astonishing episode in the life of St. Thérèse of Lisieux. It gives evidence of her genius, which has rarely been equalled. It was of course a disconcerting type of genius, whose style is sometimes overly sweet, and which has given rise to rather banal stories. Nevertheless her genius is comparable to that of Pascal.

St. Thérèse recounts a very simple story, which vividly points up her transformation, that victory of viewpoint when it comes from faith, when it comes from the very love of God and is raised to the level of such love.

TO LOOK AS GOD LOOKS

She was with her sisters, at Carmel, during an afternoon of work, sitting around a table sewing. The sister on duty at the gate arrived and asked St. Thérèse to replace her at the gate. For a Carmelite, to have an afternoon of relaxation at the gate is rather enjoyable; there one is in contact with the outside world and for someone cloistered this is rather pleasant. St. Thérèse knew that the sister next to her was very eager to go to the gate. Thus she devised a very simple stratagem: she very slowly folded up her work. The other sister then took advantage of the situation to arrange her own work very quickly, got up, and said: "Ah! Sister Thérèse, it

is clear that you are not in a hurry to render service."
And she headed for the gate. St. Thérèse did not say
anything, but later wrote: "Since that day (and that says
a great deal about the transformation of a point of view),
I never dared to judge anyone."

What would we have done? With a little less virtue,
we would have given ourselves the big role and said:
"Sister So-And-So, it would do you good to relax, so go
to the gate in my place." With a little more virtue, we
would have found the stratagem to slowly fold up our
work, but in view of the insult (sustained in the community) we would have said: "What, I render you a
service and that's all you have to say?" St. Thérèse did
not say anything. "From that day on, I never dared to
judge anyone." She had transformed her way of looking
at things. Thereafter she looked at things with an absolute trust, refusing to judge. And let us not talk here of
resignation. St. Thérèse remained extraordinarily lucid
about the defects of the community, her priory, her
fellow sisters, and herself. This is not what is involved.
No, she had raised her look to the level of the universe,
to the level of Christ's point of view, which henceforth
became her own.

In the history of mankind, this grace of faith was
given witness by someone else before St. Thérèse: a
woman, before the apostles, before the incomprehension
of the disciples, before the executioners. A woman stood
up to show us just how far the struggle of darkness and
light went. She stood beside the cross on which they
had hung, nailed, and crucified the light: it was the
Virgin, Mary.

And what do you do, what do we do about our way of looking at things? Is there this corner of darkness, this rancor, this being, this reality before which we do not want to transform our way of looking at things, which we refuse to faith, to Christ's look, to the light?

During Easter night, the Church utters two very simple words, which encompass the most unusual gift that can be announced to man: when, thinking of the baptized, and therefore of each of us, the Church solemnly promises men a childhood, an *eternal youth,* an eternally new look.*

CONCLUSION

THREE VICTORIES OVER FEAR

The Forty-Year-Old Man

To explain the nature of our distress, Péguy describes the man who is forty years old: "The misery of man, or rather the distress of man, and above all a certain taste of distress: consider the man who is forty years old. Forty years before, he had the most natural method of communication known to man, yet it is the most hermetically preserved. He knows, and he knows that he knows. He

* We hope that in reading this chapter, the reader will remember the encounter between Christ and the Samaritan woman, as reported by St. John in chapter III of his gospel; The chapter also encourages us to reread the episode of the man born blind (in chapter IX of the same gospel).

knows that since the time of man no one has ever been happy. And yet he has only one thought. And it is the thought of a foolish person. He wants his son to be happy. He thinks only of this, that his son should be happy."

"The thought of a foolish person. . . ."
Why must we Christians so
often be tempted to avoid what is bothering us?
We are clever enough
to ridicule the realities of life as
soon as they become too difficult.
To forget them,
we have alibis,
ideas,
or consoling thoughts.
Or else we talk.
We are clever in talking "about" things,
death,
sin,
or God.
We always seem to have ideas.

Let us cite the following letter, which does not offer a dissertation "on the subject of," but which tells us something about distress, directly.

"Dear Father,

There are men and women, young and old, who have recognized Christ, whose life, since that encounter, is a perpetual compromise and who know that they will always be the "rich young man." For all such people, there does not exist the happiness of believing, but the despair of believing."

This is all the letter said. It is serious because it is true.

We are quick to give ourselves reasons for not thinking of distress, for avoiding the foretaste of panic before the future, before our destiny, or more simply before fear. We would be the first to say that basically fear and distress are not Christian sentiments. This is perhaps true, but we must understand why.

Children and Fear

Christ never promised that faith would simplify things or that it would remove fear. He never promised that we would not experience distress. He promised us victory, but he did not promise us the absence of struggle.

Periodically men try to explain the origin of fear and anxiety. An important experiment was once made in Montreal, in a children's clinic near the University. The question was asked: What causes man to be afraid if he has not been forewarned? Before what does he necessarily experience fear? In the experiment children were put with animals, for example, with serpents. Being non-conditioned, they were not afraid. There are only two things before which the child is afraid, and they are important to note: a violent noise, or the loss of balance, the unknown, or insecurity. A child who falls into water is not afraid of water, but he is afraid because he no longer has a means of support. Though adults, we too experience fear. It would be pointless to think otherwise.

Let us take three examples, which seem inevitable. (There are other reasons for fear in our lives, but these three are not reserved to the Christian; every man experiences them.) Before each, let us raise this question: What difference does it make to have faith? This will require us to specify at the same time the concrete diagnostic of truth, the healthy status of our faith, and the real areas where, thanks to it, a victory is proposed for us.

Before the future,

Before others,

Before failure and sin,

What difference do Christ and the faith make?

TOO SLOW OR TOO RAPID

We cannot be indifferent toward the future. Time passes too slowly or else too rapidly. When a person has brothers and sisters, it is striking to see the difference in temperaments: there are the impatient ones or the temporizers. "An hour is long when you are waiting for the one you love. It is too short when that is all that is left to live...." The future stimulates our imagination, and undoubtedly you dream of vacations at Christmas or Easter or the month of July. At the same time it sometimes overwhelms us. We are afraid. Then we fall back on what can give us security; for example, on our work, which gives us something to hold on to, something with which to plan, to control the future, and to guarantee our tranquility. When it was decided in Sweden that cars would proceed on the right instead of on the left, a study was made whereby the organizers of the study were able in advance to calculate very closely (the aftermath proved them right) the number of accidents that this change in traffic would lead to. Having made the calculation, people then felt secure.

What is true is that there are instances where this is less easy. When in a family a person presents his fiancée to his brothers and sisters, it is always interesting to listen to the remarks: "She has a sophisticated appearance; she seems intelligent." Or: "She is not very pretty, but she will make a good housewife." Or: "She does not seem very accommodating, eh?" But then, twenty years later, things have not necessarily turned out as foreseen. There have been other virtues and other defects.

A Moment Become Sacred

What effect do faith and the presence of Christ have on this fear which we may have before the future? Contrary to the impression sometimes given by Christians, faith does not object to this struggle for security. Nor does it object to work. With far more forcefulness, faith stresses *the seriousness of the present moment.* As we say in our prayer: "... now and at the hour of our death." These are the two moments that count. But the only one we have in our possession is the present moment, *now.* Faith tells us that the present moment is much more important than we think; the present task counts much more than we suppose, for it has become something sacred. The struggle has become infinite *because we are no longer alone in leading it.*

Emmanuel Mounier, who was a great fighter, expressed it in a very beautiful and precise formula: "God invents us with ourselves." There is not Providence and then me. There is not God and then us. The relationship is an inseparable one: God has entrusted the future to us, he has put it in our hands. As for the present, everything is from God and everything is from me. God invents us with ourselves and that changes everything, radically. Even if I live the present time in the same way, everything changes, for henceforth I must be afraid not of the future, but of not taking the present seriously. The future will be inevitably different, infinitely different from what we think, from what we can imagine. But the present? God expects us to take it seriously. He expects me not

to avoid my present task, in the name of all the love
that is in his plan and in the project he has entrusted me
with. It would be as wrong for a married man to
imagine the future as if he were alone (and in the case
of Providence, this is doubly so) as for a Christian to
imagine the future as if there were no God.

Doubting Not Allowed

Regarding the future, we often have a second reason
for fear; there are others, but this one inevitably
exists in our lives, namely, other people. We are afraid
of them. We are unsure as to how to take them, how
to imagine them. They are never the way we would
like them to be. We have a twofold fear: either we
are afraid of being separated from them, we are afraid
of loneliness, or we are afraid of being responsible
for them. We are well aware of the formula of all
psychologists: the withdrawal of the father, that is, that
fear in a man when he is a father, when he must be
responsible for the future of his son. The other person
is never as we would hope; sometimes he is a problem.
However, we cannot do without him. We experience
both the fear of solitude and the fear of the problem of
friendship. Other people? We avoid them or else
accuse them. What difference does faith make?

It does not work against friendship or affection.
If evidence is needed, it would be enough to cite Christ's
tears: when Lazarus died, Jesus wept. The only time
we are told that Christ wept, it was in the name of
friendship. What a powerful testimony of friendship!

No, faith is not contrary to affection. On the contrary,

it reminds us that the "other person" has an infinitely more real dimension than we think, for each one of us deserved the death of God's Son. For a Christian, there is in each man this hidden area, beyond all that we can imagine of the other person, all that we can think of him, all the doubts we can have about appearances, all the evil which we sometimes accuse him of. There is this hidden area where every man can say to God: my Father who is in heaven, our Father. . . .

John XXIII gave such strong witness to this that all of mankind was aware: at last someone took the position of refusing to have doubts about men. Fifty years after the cry: "Workers of the world, unite," this pope said: "Men of good will, whoever you may be, unite." There remains in us something of our childhood, which is worth more than we think; there is a hidden area of good will, which can spring to life again, which can be resuscitated. John XXIII showed us that to be a Christian was to refuse to have doubts about other people. Faith requires us to believe that the other person is worth more than I think, more than I imagine. That the other person also is capable of creating goodness, that he is capable of loving and being loved.

Despair Not Allowed

Let us consider a third fear which we have regarding failure and sin. It is true that we carry our past with us; whoever we are, we are no longer masters of it. The past is there. Of course, we have not necessarily done "something bad," but the influences of the past, the situations, are there. Perhaps we do not have to reproach ourselves for something specific, but we have not risen to the level where we should be. We have grown accustomed to our mediocrity; we have gotten used to making a halfhearted effort. Inadequacies have become more or less like a prison, in which we cease to think. We have become comfortable in this situation.

In the film *Modern Times,* Charlie Chaplin has a stroke of luck, which makes us understand this. He is in prison, where he is a model inmate. One day, in spite of himself (as is often the case with Charlot), he prevents the invasion of a whole band of prisoners. As a token of his appreciation, the warden of the prison offers to set him free, to release him from prison. But Charlot begs them to keep him there. For in his cell he has a radio, a small bird cage, and flowers; he is well fed and enjoys the comforts of a warm house. He has gotten very accustomed to his surroundings.

Don't we have the same attitude toward our inadequacies and our sins? And what difference does the faith or Christ make with regard to this fear that can take possession of us and before this gilded prison in which we have enclosed ourselves? We see in the Gospel that our Lord never hides sin, yet he does not take advantage of it to overwhelm us. He never leaves us alone before sin, he forbids us to see it, to think of it only in terms of what is negative, i.e., punishment. He hides nothing of their life from Mary Magdalene, the Samaritan woman, Zacchaeus; however he does not do this to intimidate them but to show them how much they are loved and how much stronger love is than fear.

What distinguishes a Christian from a non-Christian? It is not easy to say. It is something known only to God. Surely it is not only the more or less abstract way in which we imagine God. Surely it is not the possibility of escaping from the world, which would serve as a means of consolation. It is not first of all the idea of eternal life. It is something more concrete. It is a victory over fear.

Regarding the future, the Christian refuses to think of himself as being alone.

Regarding other people, he refuses to have doubts. Doubting or scorn is forbidden.

Regarding sin, he rejects despair and refuses to believe that it is definitive or absurd.

"To those who are imprisoned, everything is a wall, even an open door." Naturally, the future, other people, loneliness, solitude, and sin can cause fear. But if faith does not rescue us from all this, it is meaningless. If it does not snatch us from the very root of our fears and anxieties, and hence not in an artificial, illusory, external way, it is not worth the effort.

We do experience fear, but we know that we can fight against it and that the victory is already won. And if we do not have more faith, is it not because we have not descended enough into our fear? Christ came to bring us this liberation, this unimaginable freedom, before that which can weigh us down. He did not come to add to our chains, but to make us free. "Untie him, let him go," he said to those surrounding Lazarus, whom he had just raised from the dead.

How can we imagine the paschal mystery? Perhaps as a cortege of men climbing a mountain.

In one of his novels, Ramuz imagines a village which had become convinced that the sun would no longer rise again. And in the village there was a man who refused to believe this and who alone, during the night, went up on the hill to await the dawn, to await the rising of the sun. Because of him, the sun once again arose. What else do Christians do at Easter? We go up on the mountain to await the coming of the Light. And perhaps because of certain people the light returns.

Perhaps what men expect most from us is that we should believe that victory over fear is possible, victory over all fears, and that it is true that a person can be happy when he believes.

part 2

TO DIMINISH GOD IN NO WAY

> For thirty years, I searched for God, and
> when I opened my eyes at the end of
> this time I discovered that it was He who
> was awaiting me.

Ferid Ed-Din Attar

Share God's Outlook or
Look for Our Own Assurance?

We have the bad habit of thinking that faith is nothing else but believing that God exists. But such a faith in no way distinguishes the nonbeliever from the Christian. How many men fully admit a force that surpasses them, without being for that reason Christians? Faith is not the simple intellectual certitude about the existence of God nor even the assurance of the existence of Christ.

"I will put my eye on your heart," God said to Ezechiel. Faith is that force which comes from on high in an always contemporary Pentecost and opens our mind to God's way of looking at things. "I try to see things and beings with the eyes of Christ." A better definition of faith cannot be given. It is enough to add: "to see God with the eyes of Christ." But this new point of view is obtained after much sacrifice and humility. It is also the occasion of a great source of renewal: to be able at last to recognize the true meaning of life, including the element of sin, to be able to discover the truth of things and the best part of people, their divine part.

Let us not be surprised if the transformation of our viewpoint by faith remains for a long time centered on human problems. Sometimes Christ seems to be expected more as a help to understanding our own life than as the guide and prophet of God. It is normal to wonder about the meaning of one's life and to be sensitive to the response brought by faith rather than to be sensitive to the call to surpass our limitations, which alone justifies it in the end. One day, though, a person must realize that there is much more, that a conversion of the mind is involved, and that if he remains attached to what faith offers in the way of practical things, he remains in a middle-of-the-road position. Faith is faith only if it is much more than the simple response to a need, even though it may be a religious one.

a New Outlook

no more is there such a thing as chance

The Creed ends with these words: "I await the life of the world to come." As if the word "to believe" was not concrete enough, the word "to await" is added.

The Christian does not adhere to an idea, even though it may be well developed, of an ideal God. He has the assurance that God has a place for him each day in a plan. And this certitude transforms everything: chance, history, progress, the appearance of absurdity, everything is changed, even our attitude toward sin. Our God is a Person, a Providence.

If, when we think of heaven our thoughts appear insipid, at least by their modesty they recall a twofold truth: heaven is God's secret and the important thing is to live this secret *now*, in faith. "But we all, with faces unveiled, reflecting as in a mirror the glory of the Lord, are being transformed into his very image from glory to glory, as through the Spirit of the Lord" (2 Cor 3, 18). Man has no right to this new point of view. The Christian God is a God who has taken the initiative, who is the first one to offer himself today as on the day when his Son became man.

Faith surpasses us not only because it is a gratuitous gift, but also because of the fullness of the viewpoint which it gives us. It will make clear a constant dichotomy between God and our way of acting toward him. Of course, only after it is too late will we become aware that we have not looked at ourselves and others with the eyes of faith. But happy the dichotomy that compels us to see that we have never arrived at that point. Faith is a kind of pilgrimage.

A *Hidden God*

We

cannot   evoke

without a feeling of sadness the

ironic   statement   of   Voltaire: "God

made man in his image, but man gave it

back to him." For anyone searching for God, this

ironic statement is a reminder of one's first duty: respect. This is where we must find the secret of that kind
of will that is found among all the saints: to treat God
as God, to diminish God in no way. To know at once
that he surpasses all that we can say about him and that
he will always therefore be for us a "hidden" God.

To discover his presence and his life is first of all to
discover him as being always beyond, as "One who is
faceless," as One who himself strives to keep us away
from idolatry. God is jealous — out of love for us — of
the face that we present to him. Nothing less than God
will do. This was the whole nostalgia of the saints. And
St. John of the Cross wrote his entire work to tell us with
what means of purification this respect for God is obtained. "Let my attitude toward God correspond to something real and may it be to some degree worthy of him."

"He whom we resemble the most, he whom we resemble the least." That progression is the key to all
biblical revelation. A constant law of opposites and com-
plementary efforts to excel presides over every new
stage in this revelation. The same is true in our own
life. The one who seeks God must be aware that he will
find him only if, in his very certitude, he has the courage
to remain unsatisfied.

A Living God

The
God, who is
completely other, is at the same
time the God who is completely close
at hand. Never in the Bible does he propose
a requirement to surpass our limitations without at
the same time affirming his presence. "Yahweh," "He
whose name cannot be known," is at the same time the
God who "comes to aid of his people," the God "who is
with you."

God is first of all the one who is present because *he
sees us*. He is the one whom nothing escapes, the one in
whose presence we walk. "My eyes on you, I will be
your counsel"; "Will you at last cease to stare at me?
Will you leave me only to swallow my saliva?" asks Job.

The God who sees is also the God *who makes an
alliance,* inviting men to his service and showing himself
to be the master and conductor of events.

Vocation and the summoning to faith are not the only
signs of this alliance; each event is a sacrament of an
encounter with God. This does not mean having visions,
but being capable, through faith, of living the extraordinary within the ordinary and of reading in the banality
of things the reality of God. But this presupposes that
we seek things in God and not only God in things.

Finally, the living God is one *who gives himself*: he
is the God of "communion." Should we be surprised that
a new threshold is crossed in the discovery of God, not
only when he gives, but when he gives himself? It is
always God who takes the initiative. He loved us "first."

The Christian God is a God who comes and intervenes; it is always he who takes the first steps, who calls and who gives. If one truly searches for him, he searches for him as the key to all existence, as the One without whom nothing makes sense.

A God who

It is not without difficulty that we pass from the attitude of servant to an attitude of son. What was hard (and so important) for Israel, is equally so in each of our lives: to believe that we have everything from God and that we are loved by him as by a Father.

But how all-pervasive is our human experience of being a son if we have such difficulties in avoiding the caricatures that deform our Father's face? Whatever may be in the order of friendship, collaboration, or authority, we all must learn to purify our idea of God.

is Father

"They were yours and you
gave them to me.
The Father himself loves you
because you love me."

Since the Incarnation and
Passion of the Son of God, we are no longer alone in
addressing ourselves to God. God can no longer look at
us without seeing in us the image of his beloved Son.
This is why, as we say at Mass, we can "dare" to say:
Our Father who art in heaven. Our assurance and our
"audacity" are found in God. Christ said, "What my
Father gave me is more precious than anything and no
one can take anything from the hand of my Father."

The Son of God is no longer before us like someone
else, like an external reality which we may contemplate,
but he has become our light, affection, the way we see
things.

The gift of his Son to himself is the gift God asks of us because it is the gift he gives us, that gift which is the Holy Spirit himself. God needs our love as he needs his Son. Such a love is no longer optional, now that he has decided upon it — and he decided upon it from all eternity.

"I called you friends because everything I learned from my Father, I have made known to you." God has but one love, and when he loves he can give but that love.

> *The Father*
> *wishes to revive with us*
> *what takes place*
> *between his Son and himself.*

Such is the ultimate secret and perfection of all prayer, as it is also the marvelous accomplishment of that faith which, enabling us to traverse all of the illusory distance between ourselves and God, does not cease to enable us to share in his life.

"And hope does not deceive since God's love has been put in our hearts by the Holy Spirit who was given to us." Like fire, the Holy Spirit cannot be given to us without transforming us in his image. He is the link between the Father and the Son. He comes from the Father and the Son because they love the life that is common to them. Thus the Spirit binds us to God according to this same love and this same unity — and unites us among ourselves. To the question, "How do we recognize the Trinity?" St. John and St. Paul do not give an abstract answer. They say that living with the Spirit and praying in the Spirit enable us to reach the Three Persons, since with the Spirit we attain to communion with the Father and the Son as well as to the communion of all men with them.

Justice or Mercy?

"I do not know what you mean by your despair; one would say that you have never heard about God or about his infinite mercy. I can no longer forgive you for such feelings: I bid you to cast it aside and to remember that all the evil you have done is nothing in comparison with the fact that you are lacking in trust" (Blessed Claude de la Colombière to an abbess).

Justice or mercy? We are clever enough
to construct a double image of God and to
thus eliminate the problem which that
causes. We very easily accept the idea that God
is merciful for us and just for others.
A compromise helps us to reconcile things
by attenuating them. God is just, but not too just
because he is merciful. God is merciful, but let
us not rely on this too much,
since he is nonetheless
just.

We must not minimize the problem. In the Bible and in the lives of the saints, God appears to have two images. One is of a pitiless justice that lays claim to the last element of the debt involved: "Come to terms with thy opponent quickly while thou art with him on the way. . . . Amen I say to thee, thou wilt not come out from it until thou hast paid the last penny" (Matt. 5, 25-26). The other image is one of a mercy which appears blind in the way it erases everything, e.g., the good thief, the prodigal son, Mary Magdalene.

An abstract answer is not sufficient. We can be told that words do not have the same meaning for God and for us, but this is not enough. We will discover it the day when, for us too, divine mercy takes up where justice leaves off.

Let us recall here one of the practical rules which St. Thérèse of Lisieux left us. She who said, "I cannot fear purgatory," tried to communicate her confidence on this point to her fellow Sisters, without always succeeding perfectly. And to Sister Febronia, who was defending the rights of divine justice, Thérèse said: "Sister, you opt for the justice of God, therefore you will receive the justice of God. The soul

receives exactly

what it expects

from God." This response presents us with a decisive truth about the Christian attitude:

It is we who choose.

it is we who choose.

It is we who choose

IT IS WE WHO CHOOSE

It is we who choose.

it is we who choose.

It is we who choose.

IT IS WE WHO CHOOSE

IT IS WE WHO CHOOSE.

it is we who choose.

This is a consoling thought, although it is also quite formidable, since it is not so easy as we think to choose mercy.

We think we choose mercy because we do not ask more than to profit from it, but this is exploiting it and not necessarily choosing it. To choose mercy, we must love it, and we must do so prior to the benefits which we hope to obtain from it.

it is we who choose.

Only love believes in love. We can love mercy, and therefore choose it, only if we have with it that affinity which makes oneself merciful. This is why our Lord did not give us other signs: "Blessed are the merciful."

If we do not love mercy for itself, aside from its benefits, we discover this terrible paradox that one is not capable of choosing it even to be saved.

Such is the practical solution which is efficacious in the apparent conflict between justice and mercy: the problem ceases for those who are merciful. Indeed, if you are merciful, you have already opted for mercy and already belong in a concrete way to the family of God's love, and divine mercy is in your power.

The problem is not that justice and mercy in God are different from what they are in us. The problem is not that it is a mystery, but that this mystery irritates or disturbs us. But it irritates or disturbs us to the extent that we look for some guarantee on the side of justice, when it would be only having the *right* to mercy, instead of recognizing the divine element in the gratuity of mercy and admitting it concretely. But this is possible and easy only for the spirit who has been disarmed by mercy. "Blessed are the merciful for they shall obtain mercy."

II

THE ROLE OF MAN

Lord,
Beware of me,
I would be capable of
   finishing the Mohammedan day

St. Philip Neri

If you are in ecstasy and your brother has need of some tea, put aside your ecstasy and bring him the tea. The God you are leaving is less certain than the God you are finding.

Jean Ruysbroeck

Neither an Ideal Nor an Idol,
But the Incarnation

God becomes God for us, he can impose himself
on our conscience, only as the one without whom
everything else is inexplicable. Faith is truly a
conversion, a change that affects our entire life. As is
the case after the rapturous feeling in a person's heart
aroused by a loved one, one's whole life is changed by
it. What faith brings is first of all this new meaning
given to all our acts. Without it, certain people conclude
that there would be left nothing but illusion, the
absurd, or suicide. Not that faith gives us unusual
visions, but it does give us a new sense of the real, of
the truth of things, which compels us to avoid ourselves
no longer.

It is not without reason that Christ wanted to
consecrate family life by a sacrament. Like all
sacraments, marriage is a sacrament of faith. That is to
say that family life is an opportunity of finding out
who God truly is, and an opportunity for being unable
to do without him. Faith leads us to understand
the marvelous thoughtfulness of God who willed that
nothing in our lives should be insignificant when seen
with the eyes of faith.

Thus our professional career and our whole life are

affected by our conversion. We would be tempted
to say of our profession and of our daily life: "Blessed
profession," "blessed daily life," which compels one
who devotes himself to it (perhaps even against his will)
to bring out the best in himself.

Frequently it is only after the fact that we become
aware of the change brought by faith to all our acts.
This does not mean that our daily activity is separated
from faith. The substance of life remains identical
with its daily routine and its banality. The Christian
does not start off as a saint; he becomes so little by
little. But he *is* a man whose eyes are opened to a new
dimension, someone who is born for another world:
the present world, seen under a new light which is the
most real and most concrete of all.

A person becomes aware that there is an extra
dimension to this world. For the person who has seen
this dimension, everything is changed, even if additional
time is needed for it to take hold in his life. And
conversion is difficult: faith is, with hope, a virtue of
imperfection, of man on the march, in a state of exodus,
in a state of becoming. Its essential role is to preside
over the passage from imperfection to perfection.

A friend of Ibn-Al-Kabchi one day asked him to show him Khidr, the mysterious personage who sometimes reveals himself to mystics during a state of ecstasy, in cities or in deserts.

> I will show him to you
>   on Friday, God willing,
>   said Ibn-Al-Kabchi.

Very happy, the man then went and distributed an entire silo of wheat to the poor — for he was a rich man — and on the same day he began to pray.

Then someone knocked at his door. The servant went to see who it was and came back to report it was a beggar.

> Tell him to come back
> after my prayer, answered
> the rich man.

The day passed without any further incident. The next day he complained to his friend:

> I did not see Khidr,
>   as you promised me.
> On the contrary,
>   he was the beggar whom
>   you told to return later.

Yafii

One day, a holy man stopped at our house. My mother saw him in the courtyard, doing sommersaults to amuse the children.

— Oh! she exclaimed, he is truly a holy man. My son, you may go out to him.

He put his hand on my shoulder and said to me:

I don't know. What would you have me do?

Little boy, what do you intend to do?

No, say what you want to do.

Well, I like to play.

Then do you want to play with the Lord?

I didn't know what to say.

He added, You see, if you could play with the Lord, that would be the greatest thing that was ever done. Everyone acts so seriously toward him that he turns out to be quite unexciting. Play with God, son. He is the best kind of playmate.

Gopal Mukerji

The Glory of God Is Living Man

When God speaks through his prophets, the latter often talk of conjugal love in order to make us understand what faith is: the union of man, such as he is, with God, such as he is. Our God is the God of the Covenant. In the light of such a situation many problems find a practical, simple, and true solution.

SHOULD OUR LIFE BE A LIFE FOR GOD OR FOR US?

It is a difficult discovery to understand how much God does in our life, although we remain free. Anyone who knows how much the discovery of a friendship can change one's life is more easily aware of it. Naturally this comparison leaves intact the infinite distance that separates a human heart from the heart of God. One must undergo periods of strong purification to pass from one regime to another, without which the comparison in question will be a source of illusion rather than of enlightenment. But to accept these purifications, in the final analysis the same spirit is needed as the one necessary to undergo the doubts, sufferings, and separations of conjugal life — "because it is for him." Progress is not achieved by rejecting the person we love, but by agreeing to have less and less need of the sensible aspect of his presence. To someone who loves God, it is proposed that he not stop at past experiences, but that he advance in faith and surpass those experiences related to the psychology of the beginner. This is the test of every life with God. The point of reference must not remain a past experience, however profound it may be, so that we think we would regress if we no longer experienced the same feelings. Provided a person expects from God nothing less than himself, he is thereby led little by little to reality.

"It is from God that I await my happiness."

For anyone in love, there is no conflict between his own happiness and that of the other person, since friendship involves the desire not to separate the two. Hasn't this fact been noted by all those who have tried to trace the itinerary of the spiritual life? Whether it be, with St. Gregory of Nyssa, the vivid design of the Word of God assimilating himself to our life; with St. Bernard, the re-education of love and apprenticeship in the motives of divine friendship; with St. Teresa of Avila and St. John of the Cross, the stages of a perpetually active conversion toward submitting oneself to divine initiatives: what is always involved is an attention to the life of the Other Person because one loves him. It could have started because one loved to love. But as soon as a person believes in divine initiative, a threshold is crossed. Whatever the postponements and false steps may have been, anyone who has undergone the experience will find it hard to forget. A second conversion is in process. One has understood that the essential element was "to have been seized by someone."

To live for someone else or for oneself: this delicate balance is lived in a concrete way, directly, in the simplicity of life, by those who love God in the way in which we love another person.

When the patrician Perpetua and her slave Felicity were put in prison to be sent to their martyrdom despite their youth, Felicity was about to give birth to a child. At the moment of birth, as she was moaning in pain, one of her guards said to her: "If you cry now, what will you do in the amphitheater, when you will be in the grip of the animals?"—"No," replied St. Felicity, "now it is I who suffer, but then Another will suffer in me."

THE NEVER-ENDING PATIENCE OF JESUS

Note how God reveals himself throughout
biblical history. What unspeakable patience!
What confusion he tolerates! What slowness!
He goes through an entire lesson — he,
First Truth — to teach men, letter by letter,
something of his divine language.
He condescends to make himself ours to the point of
appearing to share our errors, espouse our
petty preoccupations or even our small quarrels.

Those who are scandalized by these procedures and
these childlike ways of doing things miss the point.
Let them reflect, and detaching themselves from
hasty judgments and pride,
let them see the progressive initiative
with which the stages are worked out
and let them profit from it all.

God supports men as they are,
while inviting them to be better;
the impulses that he gives are not harmful,
he conducts everything with patience and sweetness.
He speaks a language that will be understood.
From each one, man or group, he asks only
what he or they can do.
His rule is not absolute, but the possible.
He lives according to what he is,
speaks and acts with men while being aware of who
and what they are.

Père Sertillanges

PROVIDENCE AND GOD'S SILENCE

When God comes to us, he does so in silence. This happens in our lives as it did at the first Christmas and at the time of the Passion: a child who does not speak, an anonymous man who is crucified. Should we believe that this silence has no meaning for us? John the Baptist, Mary Magdalene, Thérèse of Lisieux, all the friends of God have known those periods when they could no longer tolerate such silence. However, not only did they accept it, they loved it.

When we love somebody, we cannot tolerate any deceit on their part. God's silence is first of all the sign of the unbelievable respect he has for us. Can we imagine God's impatience toward our insatiable desire for signs and our need to reduce him always to the level of another man? (Isn't this the true lesson of atheism for a Christian?) This is why there are sometimes in our lives those idyllic moments when, as with the Patriarchs and Moses, God speaks "as one friend to another friend." But there are also those long and confusing periods like the four centuries of exile in Egypt or the endless cross-

ing of the desert. God is always there, much closer than we think, but not like a creature. "Do not touch me," our Lord said to Mary Magdalene after his Resurrection. Let us not debate whether God is either close at hand or far away. To St. Anthony who, after a period of abandonment, asked: "Where were you, Lord, during this time?" the answer was given: "Closer to you than ever."

There is another lesson. When the Psalms say that God falls asleep (as Christ did during the storm), it is to compel us to assume the role which he reserves for us in his plan. Out of a feeling of love, God did not want to be alone in realizing his Kingdom. And to convince us of the reality of our intervention, he condemns us to freedom. God does not cease to persuade us that his Providence has given us an indispensable role. Silence is no longer only the necessary condition for hearing, but also the expectation of love, which God cannot resist. We have the power to force him to love us. Happy the silence that returns us to our original vocation!

III

THE ANXIETIES OF FAITH

Lord, my God, teach my heart
where and how it can look for you,
where and how it can find you.
Lord, if you are not within me, if
you are absent, where would I
look for you?

St. Anselm

Faith IS A CONFRONTATION

It is quite normal to react under the strain of a test or before a problem. However, before the temptation to put faith above life, we must constantly remind ourselves that a problem is not something abnormal for faith. Faith is the courage needed to overcome problems. St. John speaks of it as a victory, which presupposes that there was combat; and St. Paul goes to great lengths to point out that a crucifying struggle is involved. "Who is the conqueror of the world if not he who believes that Jesus is the Son of God?" The combat is ours, but victory is guaranteed since it is God who has achieved it.

It is not a question of wondering whether our age is better or worse than another era, but of remembering that it is the only present one, therefore the one that will determine the success of our faith.

From the beginning of history, creation poses a question. Pessimism or optimism are on this side of the true faith. It requires a continually renewed effort to achieve lucidity and a radiography of the active forces in the world that await baptism.

"Progress in the life of the new man depends on progress in the death of the old man. The world in which we must live is in a state of being developed, and we must strive to realize that development. To believe in Jesus Christ means to be in a state of tension with a world that neither is nor will be, until the end of centuries, fully Christian. On Mount Tabor, in the light of the transfigured Christ, Peter had a great desire to establish himself there and henceforth abide for eternity in the splendor of God; Jesus quickly summoned him back to the realm of the difficult life."

**If You Increase the Suffering,
Lord, Increase the Strength Too**

Amid, the many problems that gnaw at our mind,
several categories are apparent:

> **those that come from the presentation of the faith: the delays and inadequacies of the Church, the outmoded ideas of the catechism and of religious teaching, naïveté of our own religious practice;**

> > those that come from the mystery of God himself, whether we imagine him or not as being too far away: the Holy Trinity or whether we fail to appreciate his proximity: the Incarnation, the sacraments;

> **the ordinary conditions of life: overwork, fatigue, and faith itself when it is infantile;**

the problems that pertain to our destiny: evil and its punishment, death and the world beyond. On certain days we are completely overwhelmed by the evil of cancer, the anguish connected with the hydrogen bomb, or on a more mundane level the accidents that occur on the highways.

These are not abstract questions; thus they cannot have abstract solutions. When we speak about them, why do we so often forget that God is neither an idea nor an idol, but Someone who came to earth and took upon himself these questions to the point of dying for them. If there are no abstract solutions, still two things are clear: to cut ourselves off from God, to move away from the Gospel and the Beatitudes, is to remove an opportunity to see things more clearly; at the very least, it means not taking hold of every opportunity for hope. When Christ declares that "He who does the truth comes to the light," is it not to show us that the way of hope passes through the path of concrete actions?

What is certain is that each time that we refuse to add to the punishment of the world, we draw closer, without even knowing so to Him who can help us to hope. Since the coming of Christ, we know that there is a possibility of being on the side of consolation, that is, on the side of those who believe. For it is part of our faith that, in spite of all evil, man can be a "creator of goodness" and can thereby "know" God.

Before the errors of our folly, we can only hope that there is Someone to overlook them and realize that God was "foolish" enough to delegate his goodness to us and believe that we could be the Providence of our brothers.

"Lord, God, You know our sorrow better than we ourselves know it. You know how easily our timid soul gets entangled in the difficulties which it needlessly creates for itself. We beg you to allow us to perceive their inappropriateness and to disdain them. But for whatever sorrow you inflict upon us, enable us to receive it humbly from your hand, and give us the strength to bear it."

Sören Kierkegaard

THE FOOLISH THINGS OF THE WORLD
AND THE WEAK

As every biblical story and history of the Church
indicates, the conditions that are deemed little
propitious to faith or the people that are thought to
be the most poorly equipped, sometimes offer the best
evidence of divine life. "But the foolish things of the
world has God chosen to put to shame the wise,
and the weak things of the world has God chosen to
put to shame the strong, and the base things of the
world and the despised has God chosen, and the things
that are not, to bring to naught the things that are"
(1 Cor. 1, 27-28). It is at Corinth, in an area of
stevedores and laborers, and not in Athens, a center
of intellectual aristocrats, that St. Paul found the truest
understanding of and newest vigor for the Christian
faith. Is the situation different today, even within
the Church?

The first grace of faith is born in man's heart when
he discovers that he cannot suffice unto himself. It
is in the experience of his limitations that God arouses
in man his first calling, the one heard by Abraham:
"Leave your country." It is never easy to convert, by
agreeing, as the Hebrew word "faith" says, to be
borne along by someone else because he is dependable.

IV

CHRIST AND THE CHURCH ARE ONE

To help me fall
I had friends in great
    number
But to lift myself up
I found myself completely
    isolated.

St. Teresa of Avila

Impossible to Hold Firm Alone

The complaint of St. Teresa of Avila is forever true. Each of us can reflect upon the role other people have placed in our relationship with God. Is this perhaps the first way to discover the Church? And who fails to discover how difficult, if not impossible, it is to remain true and firm in his conviction when he is alone in living it? These are the reasons that dispose us to understand better the necessity of intermediaries for faith and thus to desire the help of a community and to learn to love the Church.

Anyone who thinks about intermediaries for his faith can soon be tempted by deception and discouragement.

And when we think of the Church, we sense the difficulties very quickly. As if the role of intermediaries was not to lead to something greater than they, as if the greatest benefit that a man could receive from someone who transmits the Gospel to him, was not that urgency to surpass his limitations. The essential renunciations are not the ones we choose ourselves. Certainly we would not have chosen to be deceived by those very people who transmit salvation to us. But don't the latter have to be saved first? And do we realize that their salvation also depends on us? Happy are deceptions if they require us not to give up the struggle without going farther on in our efforts, to be discontented with prejudices and hasty suspicions, and to understand better the grandeur of the message that is transmitted to us.

HAPPY PROBLEMS

To believe in the Church is to adhere to the mystery of Christ, which is found therein:

Christ comes to look for man in the midst of sin and slowly draws him away from it. This is the mystery of the fundamental plan of God, which is to give himself to the world by taking on a human flesh. God went to the limits of this plan. One can adhere to the Church, the mystery of faith, only by living it here on this earth.

How could such a life not bring suffering? The only sign of authentic achievement is the cross. The truth of all our responses can be summarized as follows: "Does a person truly love someone when he cannot suffer for him?"

The Problems Are Not of Today

Augsburg and Florence, Luther and Savonarola:
two difficult periods.

In the center of Augsburg stands the square of the
cathedral, made for Grimm's tales or Mozart's music.
One enters the cathedral: after having viewed the tran-
sept, we look upon the altar where Luther celebrated
Mass. If we continue through the city, we find a cloister,
which has become a Protestant church. A plaque on the
street reminds us that here Cardinal Cajetan, a Dominican, spent a week in theological discussion with Luther.
Sent from Rome, he came with an offer to become a
cardinal.

Fifty years earlier, another city, another church:
Santa Croce in Florence. Two legates arrive from Rome
to offer Savonarola, a Dominican, the position of cardinal, thereby trying to quiet his protests against the
dissolution of morals and faith in the Church. Savonarola
delays his answer until the next day; in the meantime,
one of the emissaries requests a woman for the night.
The next day, from the chair of Santa Maria, Savonarola
responds: "I wish no other purple than the one of my
blood." He had the other purple.

**Fifty years later
Luther rose up.**

Under St. Augustine
men waged battle
for the baptism of children.

**Bossuet went to the point
of initiating false police
reports in the court of
Louis XIV against Fenelon.**

*The Preservation of Latin
had its martyrs in England
after the Reform.*

At the Council of
Ephesus, regarding the
question of the two
natures of Christ,
bishops came to blows,
even to the point of
almost being thrown out
of windows.

AND LET US NOT FORGET THAT JOAN OF ARC
SUFFERED FROM THE MACHINATIONS
OF THREE POPES AND TWO KINGS.

**All of these people believe that they
possessed the faith. And why do we always think of the Church as an idea?**

The Church, too, is incarnate.

Reread the description of the first parish in Corinth by
St. Paul: 1 Cor., chap. 4 to chap. 11.

Before the Changing Church:
Disorder or Greater Striving?

O BE CAPABLE of not re-
gretting the beauty which a
loved one had in the past,
but to know how to discern the dynamic qualities she
enjoys today — isn't this one of the most authentic signs
of a person's maturity? What would we think of a man
who would weep before his wife, regretting that she no
longer had the appearance she had when they were en-
gaged? Isn't remaining faithful to the appearance, amid
its changing states, the privilege of love and part of its
grandeur? Aren't we sometimes asked to do this when
we look at the Church?

But would the change be only a source of disorder?
For nothing else was proposed to the apostles and the
early Christians. Christ's pedagogy toward his disciples
was clear enough: it was always one of a gradual striving. Why should we think it would be any different for
us? We note how quickly Christ wanted legal and religious guarantees, founded on observances alone or only
on the need of his presence, to be surpassed. And these
signs were put aside for another, more profound and
more demanding, loyalty.

The achievements of the Second Vatican Council
must be preserved and improved upon. To help in this
effort, we should make sure that our evangelical ferment
does not decrease in its fervor.

Those Entrusted to Us by God

"We cannot not talk," exclaims St. Peter. Dialogue is part of faith. But our Lord warned us that such dialogue was not easy: "Whoever is ashamed of me and my words, of him will the Son of Man be ashamed" (Luke 9, 26).

> We are responsible for those placed in our custody by God. My neighbor is anyone I come across in need, so that I would have to look the other way so as not to see him. "Whoever gives you a cup of water to drink . . . because you are Christ's, he shall not lose his reward" (Mark 9, 40).

For a Christian, witness is perhaps quite often the highest form of dialogue. God takes charge of the dialogue by making sure that the word of the witness is understood at the proper time. St. Paul, who had begun by sending St. Stephen to his martyrdom, understood this.

"Do you know how to make a bridge?" The question is a serious one for anyone aware of the temptation with the status quo, bourgeoisification, and the fear that stalks man. "Explain to me what your faith consists of." The answer to this reflects upon us. And God's judgment will count at least as much as the judgment of men. Do we pray enough for those who have to respond?

The best way not to be
deceived by those who reveal
the message of faith to us,
is to understand that we too are
given the duty to pass it on to others.
Let us first be loyal in our
role as witnesses of faith;
in the meantime many problems will fade away.

V

INVITED TO THE MEAL

In the true relationship of prayer, it is not God who hears what is being asked; it is the one who prays, who continues to pray to the point of himself being the one who hears what God wants.

Sören Kierkegaard

It is quite normal to be exhausted by the inadequacies of reforms, the strangeness of the vocabulary of the liturgy, the lack of know-how in some priests. Does this mean that one should sulk over religious practices and the sacraments? It would be quite unusual that at a time when men are rediscovering in their secular life the necessity for practice (under a thousand forms), Christians are abandoning the idea.

Is what we feel on Sunday morning something artificial? This immense need within us to redevelop the unity of our life, to avoid the fragmentation which most of us are forced to undergo, and beyond that, the need to meet someone who loves us, waits for us, someone who says that we are not alone in our struggle, our hope, our failures, our weaknesses. Christ is always there to receive us. He offers us this encounter in the sacraments. God comes to us in the sacraments the way Christ came to us at the first Christmas, as a very poor child who needs us in order to share his divine energy with us within the actions of our life. To a degree he offers us a form of cooperation with him.

Accepting the sacraments means first of all agreeing to be sought out by God and accepting the opportunity offered us by Christ to rejoin God.

Practice enables man to discover that he is not alone in his existence, that Someone awaits him, and that his life is a twofold act. It suggests to man that he should not be merely a spectator, but a co-worker in his destiny. This is the great novelty of Christianity, as St. Paul proclaimed it: "We are co-workers with God." God gives us our freedom so that we may use it at each moment of our great human experiences:

> before evil, with penance;
> > before human love, with matrimony;
> > before fatherhood, with baptism;
> before the struggle against the anguish of death,
> with the sacrament of the sick;
> > before the responsibility for our brothers,
> > with confirmation and holy orders.

Face to face with all these great experiences, we are led to be co-workers in humble, day-by-day, coherent acts, for example, in sharing the meal with the friends of Christ.

TOO MUCH DUST ON THE LITURGY

It is true that present-day reforms are inadequate and that a great effort is involved in giving dignity to our "practice." But this is a problem of riches, or rather of false riches. Isn't this our case when we do not feel sufficient need for enlightenment, salvation, and faith to live?

Let us recall the mail delivery from Stalingrad, the last one that could leave the city by plane before the surrender. These extraordinary letters, confiscated by the German command staff and found after the war, were written by men who were condemned either to death or to imprisonment. What can we learn from them? We note the letter of the young husband to his wife describing the color of the curtains he would like on the windows and suggesting a place for the crib of the child she is expecting. The letter of the pianist whose fingers were frozen. The awesome letter of the son of a general, in which the son expresses his complete hatred for his father, accusing him of being responsible for the war and for what is happening to him. And then there is the letter of the priest: ". . . The night before Christmas, eleven comrades celebrated the birth of Christ in a hut. It was not an easy thing to gather them together from among the band of

disabused, hopeless, and cynical men. But those I found
came voluntarily. There are many altars in this vast
world, but certainly not one poorer than this one.
Yesterday again, men gather together around a box
where I put the gray-green jacket of a comrad fallen
in combat. I read extracts from the gospel of St. Luke.
I gave them communion under the form of black
bread, representing the body of our Lord, and implored
God's grace and mercy for them. But I did not speak
of the fifth commandment. . . . The men were seated
on piles of wood, their eyes directed toward me."

Those men did not wonder if they needed practice.
They did not have the arguments of modern-day
progressives. They did not have the arguments of false
riches. They did not wonder if the service was to be
said in Latin or in German. They needed the only two
things man cannot give himself: the body of Christ
and the forgiveness of his sins. And all of a sudden
they would rediscover the truth of their assembly,
the truth that before an absolute distress there was
Someone who would be their companion in very
simple acts: gathering together, breaking bread, talking
with one another. That would give them hope even
in the face of death, even in the face of the most terrible
doubt.

MOMENTS WORTH A LIFETIME

What would a priest say if he were asked what the sacraments bring him? No doubt, he would say that they do not bring him anything and that at the same time they bring him everything and that he would not exchange certain moments of his priestly life for anything else in the world.

Thus, when one is offering Mass in a church, at the moment when he gives Christ's blessing at the end, there is, as it were, an immense joy, no doubt unique, that of seizing all at once all those lives in front of him and being able to unify them. Perhaps the people are preoccupied during the Mass. It's hard to know. But what an incredible thing to be able, above and beyond their problems, and even dissensions, to give back life to the best part of them. What an unbelievable thing to be unified once again before Christ.

Nor would one give away that moment in confession when, above and beyond the monotony and banality of the lists of sins, and in spite of the temptation he sometimes may have to put a sign on the outside of the confessional, "Sinners Wanted," he discovers all of a sudden an expression of truth, a moment of light, an extraordinary good will. Then one feels an urge to get down on his knees, for he has been the witness of reconciliation between a man and himself. Isn't reconciling a person with himself, through the blessing of Christ, worth an entire life?

Finally, there is another moment in his sacerdotal life that a priest would not give away at any price, the one when he is called to the aid of a man who has just discovered that the sickness he is afflicted with is a serious one and that it can lead to death. The sick man calls, extends his hand, and in the name of Christ is brought the strength and life provided by the anointing of the sick. And when the priest leaves, the situation is reversed: it is Christ who henceforth holds his hand, who restores his confidence and hope, appealing to the noblest part of his being. Such moments would not be given away for anything else in the world inasmuch as it is through them that the priest understands more clearly to what extent God is communion.

Lead, Kindly Light

Lead, Kindly Light, amid the encircling gloom,
    Lead Thou me on!
The night is dark, and I am far from home
    Lead Thou me on!
Keep Thou my feet; I do not ask to see
The distant scene — one step enough for me.

I was not ever thus, nor prayed that Thou
    Shouldst lead me on;
I loved to choose and see my path, but now
    Lead Thou me on!
I loved the garish day, and, spite of fears,
Pride ruled my will: remember not past years.

So long Thy power hath blest me, sure it still
    Will lead me on,
O'er moor and fen, o'er crag and torrent, till
    The night is gone;
And with the morn those angel faces smile
Which I have loved long since, and lost awhile.

JOHN HENRY NEWMAN